•BEAUTiFUL COUNTRY

*Earthly Meditations: New and Selected Poems*

*Lives of the Animals*

*Reign of Snakes*

*In the Bank of Beautiful Sins*

*What My Father Believed*

*Moon in a Mason Jar*

*The Sinking of Clay City*

# BEAUTiFUL COUNTRY

ROBERT WRIGLEY

PENGUIN POETS

PENGUIN BOOKS
Published by the Penguin Group
Penguin Group (USA) Inc., 375 Hudson Street, New York, New York 10014, U.S.A.
Penguin Group (Canada), 90 Eglinton Avenue East, Suite 700, Toronto, Ontario, Canada M4P 2Y3
(a division of Pearson Penguin Canada Inc.)
Penguin Books Ltd, 80 Strand, London WC2R 0RL, England
Penguin Ireland, 25 St Stephen's Green, Dublin 2, Ireland (a division of Penguin Books Ltd)
Penguin Group (Australia), 250 Camberwell Road, Camberwell, Victoria 3124, Australia
(a division of Pearson Australia Group Pty Ltd)
Penguin Books India Pvt Ltd, 11 Community Centre, Panchsheel Park, New Delhi – 110 017, India
Penguin Group (NZ), 67 Apollo Drive, Rosedale, North Shore 0632, New Zealand
(a division of Pearson New Zealand Ltd)
Penguin Books (South Africa) (Pty) Ltd, 24 Sturdee Avenue, Rosebank, Johannesburg 2196, South Africa

Penguin Books Ltd, Registered Offices:
80 Strand, London WC2R 0RL, England

First published in Penguin Books 2010

10  9  8  7  6  5  4  3  2  1

Page 93 constitutes an extension of this copyright page.

LIBRARY OF CONGRESS CATALOGING IN PUBLICATION DATA
Wrigley, Robert, 1951–
Beautiful country / Robert Wrigley.
p. cm.—(Penguin poets)
ISBN 978-0-14-311837-4
I. Title.
PS3573.R58B43 2010
811'.54—dc22    2010025620

Printed in the United States of America
Set in New Caledonia
Designed by Ginger Legato

Special thanks to the Rockefeller Foundation for
a residency at the study center in Bellagio, Italy,
during the fall of 2007, where some
of these poems were begun.

*for Bob Burns and Dennis Lockwood*

# CONTENTS

BEAUTiFUL COUNTRY

 *"This is a beautiful country."*

—John Brown, seated on his coffin, as he rode to the gallows,
December 2, 1859

# Responsibility

*for Clyde Fixmer*

At the lower fence line under the stars
he hears what at first he takes
to be the neighbor's mare,
come to investigate his apple pocket,

but then gets that neck-chill
and knows otherwise and turns
to see by starlight alone a dust devil
spitting along perpendicular to the wire

and straight at him. He's seen thousands
of the things but never crossed paths
with one on foot, and watches
as long as he can before the grit

of its coming edge gets in his eyes.
Then up his pants legs and sleeves
the dust of it spins. His shirt wants to open
over his spine, his cap levitates

and vanishes, the fence buzzes
and rattles, its staples scraping, its posts
making a knuckle-crack clatter—
and then it's past, back-and-forthing

over the pasture toward the hulk
of the old stable, from the roof of which
it removes three or four thin flimsy shakes
and causes the aged gelding BJ

to flinch and whirl and trot out into the open
and glare, with stars in his eyes,
at the man who is responsible
for everything that happens.

## County

County of innumerable nowheres, half its dogs
underfed and of indeterminate breed. County
of the deep fryer and staples in glass against mice,
county of horned gods and billed hats. Sweat county,
shiver county. The hallowed outhouse
upholstered in woolly carpet, the sack of lime,
time out of time, county of country music.

Insufficient snowplows county, county
of the blasted doe all winter in a drift, dust sift
and feather duster county, county of the quo
all status is attached to. Of batches and bitchdogs
howling, of rowels and boots, of soot wash,
of the chimney sweep's red beard,
of the songless radio preaching to no one in the shed.

County of the deadly road, of the shoat pig roasted
in a pit. County of molasses, hobo coffee,
and sugarless soft drink, county of the methamphetamine
picture window, of the padlock and massive hasp.
County of tools and dewormers. Currycomb
and salt block, black pepper gravy, red-eye venison,
blood sausage, county of Bud Light girl posters.

Treble hook county, chum county, bear bait
and dead wolf county. County of the coyote pelt
nailed to the barn door. Bruised woman county,
of men missing one or more fingers, single-finger
wave county. Pistol alongside the cash register.

Pitch-dense firewood county, county of the fearful
and fearless, of the distant mysterious school.

Target-poor county, Walmart holy land,
malodorous pulp mill and paper plate county.
County of the hundred-yard drive to the post office,
oddly familiar faces among the wanted posters,
four-hour drive from the county seat county,
unadopted highway, county of no return.
County of August always somewhere burning.

Beer can bejeweled barrow pit county, hardly
one bullet-unpunctuated county road sign county.
County of the ATV and ancient Indian trail
into the high mountains. Get your bull or buck
county. On-the-way-to-somewhere-else,
do-si-do, hundred frozen casseroles
after the funeral, go to heaven county,

blister and blister rust county, Yahweh trailer-house
county, unassisted living, county
of the Gospels and the *Penthouse* under the bed.
County of tenderness and terror, of almost
universal skepticism, Jesus country county.
County of the cell tower stipend, everywhere
and anywhere, boneyard county, county

a day's drive from the end of the open road.
Softshell Baptist county. Pentecostal pancake county.
County of illusions and of hard facts. Rock

and broken shock, rock and roll aught-six
save your shell casing. County of not quite breathtaking
vistas, of the for sale sign, of timothy and brome,
spring and autumn slaughter county, meat county, home.

# Hay Day

Beautiful, the nine-hundred-pound round
bale of smooth brome the grower and I roll
from the back of his truck against the usual tree.
The horses can hardly contain themselves.
They smelled and came running across the field
and now they look and nicker, and move in
even before I can cut loose the four long
bands of twine from the edge, where they nip instead
the greenest, sweetest stuff from the wound center
of the man-high wheel of it. They feed there
for most of an hour, long after I've written the check
and the hay man's made his way back home,
and it being August, I relax on the porch
with a beer my wife brought from town
and, knowing my usual routine on such days, slipped
into the freezer until just minutes ago, so that
I might sit and watch the horses, having had
all they want, move in slow circles around
the great black walnut's vast expanse of shade,
then stop—BJ, the troublesome elder, and Red,
the elegant, genuinely exceptional ride—
as always in the same precise relation to one another
(Red at forty-five degrees and a little back)—
before taking off around the fence line
at a trot, then a canter, and then, for just a few
beautiful moments, a dead and joyful run.

# Introduction to Poetry

Here is the studious, would-be poet, in April 1973,
leaned against a bee-mad blossoming silver maple tree,

middle of the greeny quad, the State University
of Southern Nowhere, and reading Herrick with much perplexity.

Then *liquefaction* happened. He said it aloud and the word arose
as poetry, although so did Julie, streaking by without her clothes.

Julie, whose sweet flows were yesterday in class a mystery,
but which now, along with his life's work, he could see.

## Every Night the Long Swim

I miss her, the old dog
dead now more than four years.

She was black and used to dream dreams
that bubbled to the surface of her as she slept.

She preferred the water to the land.
She loved a hand and the way it might be held

from the arm of the chair into the daily air she lived in,
though this world was a long, dry lakelessness

no one in the household but she was so ungilled for.

Thus her dreams.
                    Always she seemed to be running,
though I think now she was afloat, and every day

was the duck she offered us. Every night the long swim
over water so dark she disappeared and became the dream,

then swam back, rising,
                    shaking away the night into the light
until it was gone.

## Sisyphus Bee

I couldn't help it, I nearly fell asleep
on the grass in front of the tulips,
but lying there seemed to be
the best angle from which to see
and study the way the bee

worked from red lip to lip,
his legs by the third filled up
and by the fourth so heavy he
fell from the blossom onto me,
and I let him rest easy

for a while, though he slipped
on my belly hair and sipped
at a drop of sweat, maybe—
he was, it seemed, so thirsty—
then walked the half-length of me,

or of my torso at least, a trip
that cost him each step
a milligram of the load we
both knew was his goal and misery,
and how it was he'd come to be,

of all unflowery places, on me,
though in the sun I could also see
his long trail up my belly,
and the gold left behind each step,
before he flew, awkwardly,
to the next waiting tulip.

# Fraternity

In consideration of his age, the sheriff would not cuff
the old man Burdette, who'd arrived with the body
of his twin brother bound in wire
in the bed of the truck, a penny-size new mouth dead
center of the forehead, nothing much at all
underneath the crown's sparse hair.

But then, the sheriff could never tell one brother
from the other, except when he'd asked.
Leaning on the rusty fender, he peered
at the sad old eyes, the wedge of pale face gaped
with shock, the bird-claw hands tied in his lap,
a black sulfuric flare over the back of a knuckle.

"Now which one are you?" asked the sheriff, looking down.
"Me?" said the live one, smiling. Then touching
the dead one's waxen lip, the sheriff said, "No. I mean,
which one's this?" The autumn light at midday
made Main Street a boulevard in heaven,
but for a tumbleweed and the neon sign reading "-rue Value."

"Why, that there," the old man said, "is Nils. Finest brother
the world ever know'd, and I'm the one what kilt him."
In the chill of the metal bed, the brother's blood
was almost black. The sheriff eyed a cloud's reflection there.
"He was always the sad one, wasn't he?" asked the sheriff.
"Always down about this or that or nothing."

The smile again. Why wouldn't it all be true?
And would it matter if it were not?

"You could never stop smiling yourself, could you?
And now you're all alone."
Then the smell of an opened body, part metal,
part sweat. "I s'pose that's true," said the old man.

Then, again, he smiled. And anyone who could have said
whose smile was whose was also dead.
So the sheriff said, "Come on, let's go," and took him
by the arm who said his name was Nelson Burdette
until the day he died and was buried by his brother's side,
a killer and a fratricide.

## Poor Priscilla

They bought a pup
            and put it on a chain
and never let it off again.
            It barked and snarled for years that way.
I was a child and feared
            the dog for the children
it seemed to want to bite, and for all
            the times I might have been bitten by it,
though I wanted most of all to set it free.
            I thought with stovepipe leggings,
welder's gloves, and a catcher's mask
            that I'd contrived a way to do so,
though I'd forgotten—I did not realize
            until too late—both my feet
and my ass, the wound
            on the latter of which required
some stitches but resulted,
            as what luck I had would have it,
in the dog's freedom after all.
            Some hard-core uncle's farm
it had gone to, no doubt,
            though recently my mother
revealed to me that that wasn't it
            at all. Turned out those neighbors
just killed the dog themselves
            and left it on our porch
as evidence of what
            she could not imagine.
"I had not thought of them
            for years," she went on.

It seems my father took the dog
        and buried it, and did I know
"before the dog they'd had a girl once,
        also named Priscilla,
who'd been eaten by some hogs?"

## Lichen

Not moss, but slower, a kind of *lumpenproletariat*
fungus comes in bunches no one keeps an eye on.
Grandmother ones, grandfathers, though where they're at
they're babies, half-birthed among a thousand tiny generations.

And lacy they are, tightly massive as minimal forests,
but always more amazing the closer you look.
And holding the dew in billions of pinprick droplets,
they drink their fill and wait, the very name meaning *to lick*.

## I Like the Wind

We are at or near that approximate line
where a stiff breeze becomes
or lapses from a considerable wind,
and I like it here, the chimney-smokes
right-angled from west to east but still
for those brief intact stretches
the plush animal tails of fires.
I like how the stiffness rouses the birds
right up until what's considerable sends them
to shelter. I like how the afternoon's rain,
having wakened the soil's raw materials,
has sent a root-smell into the air around us,
which the pine trees sway stately within.
I like how the sun strains not
to go down, how the horizon tugs gently at it
and how the distant grain elevator's shadow
ripples over the stubble of the field.
I like the bird feeder's slant
and the dribble of its seeds. I like the cat's
sleepiness as the breeze then the wind
then the breeze keeps combing her fur.
I like the body of the mouse at her feet.
I like the way the apple core I tossed away
has browned so quickly. It is much to be admired,
as is the way the doe extends her elegant neck
in its direction, and the workings of her black nostrils too.
I like the sound of the southbound truck
blowing by, headed east. I like the fact
that the dog is not barking. I like the ark
of the house afloat on the sea of March

and the swells of the crop hills bedizened
with cedillas of old snow. I like old snow.
I like my lungs and their conversion
to the gospel of spring. I like the wing
of the magpie outheld as he probes beneath it
for fleas or lice. That's especially nice,
the last sun pinkening his underfeathers
as it also pinks the dark when I close my eyes,
which I like to do, in the face of it,
this stiff breeze that was,

when I closed them, a considerable wind.

# Progress

You begin to fear all the nowheres are somewheres now.
Everywhere's been discovered. Is there anywhere you can go
and find a hair-netted octogenarian wrangling a walker
and four massive, camp-size cast-iron skillets full

of Sunday dinner fried chicken at 9:00 a.m.
and ask if she's serving breakfast, then have her say,
"Sure thing, hon, but you'll have to wait on yourselves"?
Remember how pretty you were? Well, your sweetheart was

beautiful, and all you wanted was some
sunny-side up eggs and bacon with hash browns,
a white boat of peppery pan gravy,
and a mason jar of homemade apple butter

you'd have to pry the disk of wax out of
and dollop on your toast with a long-handled teaspoon.
These days Main Street features two antiques emporia,
a coffee shop, and a wine store offering Friday-night

tastings of the latest regional Cab Franc cuvée.
The café's become an office dealing in view lots,
weekend lakeside rentals, and time-share condominiums.
That was twenty-five years ago, you tell yourself.

The old chicken-frying woman probably never saw
what's become of the place, though what with the baskets
of brightly colored artificial geraniums hanging
from the vintage lampposts and the new pocket park

with a memorial to the loggers of yesteryear,
she'd probably approve. There's a new high school too,
and according to its electronic marquee sign,
not only is there a girls' basketball team, but they've won

the state three-B championship for the second time this year.
And probably the granola and yogurt breakfast parfait
with seasonal fruit from California's Central Valley
you had this morning was better for your arteries anyway.

Your sweetheart's still gorgeous, and you're willing
to settle for distinguished or fairly well preserved,
but the jam this morning comes in those tiny single-serving jars
sealed with a stirrup of foily paper, and you remember

how that morning's apple butter was explosive with cinnamon
and cloves, how the tang came from the cooked-
to-submission red and golden mottled peelings,
and how the old lady wheeled and toddled

over to the kitchen doorway and called you back to
"try this for a finish up," and it was a plank of sweet cream
strudel still warm from the oven, a perfect square of butter
liquefying itself on top, and you and your sweetheart split it

and because of it all fell more deeply in love than before,
and after paying the ridiculously tiny bill and thanking
the kindly cook, drove up the lake road and found
a perfect spot in what is now an eighteen-hole, pro-designed

golf course, and made love on a grandmotherly quilt,
within a body's length of the cold, clear water,
and lay there for an hour in the sun, as naked and at ease
as no one in that place will ever be again.

# Miss June, 1971

Many hours it had taken me, tapping with the heel
of a combat boot on the butt end of a pocket knife,
to etch the dime-size circle on one of my dog tags,
then a vertical dissecting line across its diameter
and two smaller legs from midway to the circumference:
a peace sign to the right of my name, service number, O-
negative blood type, and "Protestant," my religious preference,

this last, the part I remain most bewildered by now, having none
at any point in my life, but being in those days unaware
it could have been a choice, that I could have chosen to be a Jew
or a Hindu, or even Catholic, which might have gotten me
into the pants of one of those dark-haired local Italian girls
I mooned for so relentlessly in my predraft days.

Daily a deuce-and-a-half truck pulled up outside
the barracks and left to dispense a dozen of us
two-by-two to the host of brainless details
contrived to make us useful: COs, gays,
bed wetters, the strangely too violent to be trusted
with guns. That day, cool and serene Devereaux and I
were to scrub the floors of the Nursing Command Center.

That was how I came to be on my knees under the desk
of an oddly smallish command sergeant major,
in such a position that my dog tags slipped from my shirt,
so that when I rose, dizzy with ammonia fumes,
they dangled over the front of my fatigues,
and when the sergeant spotted my handiwork,
he seized the tags and used the chain to pull my face

within a fist's width of his and spit his opinions at me.
I was, I recall, a goddamned coward,
the symbol was the footprint of the American chicken,
and he had half a mind to write me up on charges
of defacing army equipment. There was more, of course,
involving the men he said he'd lost,
the chain of command, the shame of my parents,

the Stars and Stripes, and the USA itself, which clearly
I did not love and should therefore simply leave.
I stared into his left eye. The thing is, none of them
frightened me by then, and anyway I did not disagree
with anything he said. As far as I could tell,
my cowardice had everything to do with *not* leaving,
not firmly and insistently removing his hands from me

and walking out the door, through the gates of the base
into the balmy Texas afternoon and heading north.
But there was—and I admit the strangeness of the memory—
between his lower two front teeth a tiny dark
green spot of parsley or lettuce that caught my eye
and held it all through the rest of his harangue.
It made me think that, like Devereaux, I could also be

a vegetarian, could abhor the killing of any fleshed thing
and thereby give my objection all the more
conscientiousness, although the look he gave me also made me
imagine the haymaker punch I could have laid him out with.
About that, in truth, I was a coward too. My mind

wandered. I wanted desperately to be a smoker
but couldn't do it. Even the pantywaist Tareytons

I tried made me sick. We used to give our soldiers
free cigarettes, and last week I read that some prude
of a legislator wants to disallow them *Playboy*. Which occurs
to me now because there was then, on the wall above
the sergeant's desk, the foldout of Lieko English, Miss June,
1971. She had an Asian-seeming first name,
so I wondered about the wartime myths—

those sixteen-year-old hooch girls you could have and have—
but here was this lifer sergeant, not smallish really
but in fact a tiny man, two full heads shorter than I.
I'd been looking down at his eyes and now looked
nearly floorward, over his girlish left hand
knotted in my dog tag chain, and over his quivering,
enraged lower lip, at the speck of green there,
lodged between his diminutive lower teeth.

She straddled a rough split rail fence. An assistant
or two would have helped her into place,
as she carefully nestled her lovely, flawless inner thighs
around the splintered wood. That would be a job
I could do, I remember thinking. Not the daily collection
in the deuce-and-a-half, but in a Mercedes, say,
or at worst a van filled with camera gear

and the promise of pulchritude at an hourly wage.
*Pulchritude.* I was twenty years old and knew that word
and probably knew it because of *Playboy*,
which had also taught me *ribald* and *fellatrix* and the legend
of the stars on the cover's *P*, and the great good fortune
of Hugh Hefner, who was, as the sergeant might have known,
one of those we were supposed to be fighting for, and why,

along with Lieko English, red meat, and the distant possibility
of fellation. Which, alas, was when it dawned on me
that the one time I'd been so lucky was with a girl
just about the size of the sergeant himself. Paula
was her name and she's dead now and so,
given his middle age then, is the sergeant major
probably, and even Lieko English is, like me,

in her late fifties, old enough, perhaps, to have a son, or even
a grandson, in the army. My O-negative makes me a universal donor.
I was not a Protestant then and did not protest
the sergeant major's treatment of me. Instead, I took it
and didn't say a word but studied
the bit of parsley between his teeth, August 1971,
and, for many years thereafter, understood nothing.

## Misunderstanding

They've made love in the woods again
and now she's asleep, her head on his belly,
and he only wants to study her as she naps.

But the black carpenter ant, the one he's watched
climb the curve of her right breast,
now wanders from the pinkish aureole borderlands

in spirals round and round and round again,
which is why he reaches as carefully as he can
and plucks the ant up and flicks it back to the forest,

apologizing at just the moment she opens her eyes
and almost frowns, then closes them, and allows herself
to sleep again, although he was talking to the ant.

## Anthropomorphic Duck

Every morning, the solitary blue-winged teal drake
swam the east-to-west length of the high mountain lake
in silence. Every evening he'd fly back,
uttering on his way a single sad quack.
What we wondered, my sons and I, was why.

Why here, an otherwise duckless nowhere? The sky
was wide and blue above him; surely the flyways beckoned.
Though we also knew we had no way of reckoning
what kind of inner life he might have possessed,
if inner life is what instinct is, or if he was lost,

or if—and this, we understood, was as much about ourselves—
there was something he himself had lost. Was our blue wing
blue because, like certain geese, his kind mates for life?
This was how we came to refer to her as his wife,
as Mrs. Teal, the missing one, for whom he mourned,

whose absence had lead him, with the terrible wound
of his grief, to come to this place of refuge and learn
—well, what? To be a duck again, since our theory'd turned
him into something else? The last morning, my sons climbed
a nearby peak on their own, and I passed the time

alone and was, after an hour that way, so lonely
I could find no escape. I wanted nothing, except to have them
back with me, and then I saw Mr. Teal on his morning swim.
He was stopped not far from camp. I knew it was him,
though he was ass-up among some reeds

in the shallows. I watched him feed
for a long time, just the two of us, until I was hungry
and ceased for a little while to worry.
And later, when the boys came back, he took again to the sky,
uttering as he did his single inconsolable cry.

# Letting Go

There is no blue like this mountain lake's.
A breeze stirs along the surface
a silver filigree that makes it even bluer.
A remnant snowfield has shed
a few bergs along the northern shore,
and the single tiny island of stone and three
subalpine fir trees appears mythological,
an upland, since it's in the middle
of the lake's cold depths, likely never
to have been set foot on by a man.

The younger of the sons cannot quite
process it all yet, having collapsed
almost in tears, not because he has arrived
at last, but because his father, wracked
with his years and with cramps, gagging
all the last five hundred vertical feet,
is still standing, despite it all.
The three of them—two sons and their father—
will spend three days there, and none of them
has ever been to a more spectacular place.

What's left of the day is only more work:
pitching of the tents, erection of a cook shelter,
the building of a fire pit, hanging
the hammock and a strung line
to drape their sweat-soaked walking clothes on.
Then an icy dip, all the rime and soil
sloughed off, and just as night begins
the preparation of the evening meal—

a can of chicken, an onion, six garlic cloves,
and two boiled three-serving bags of rice.

It is the next morning, in the sun
of the new day, sore now from both the walk in
and from the first night's sleep on the ground,
that they each and together begin to see
where it is their toil has brought them.
A pair of mountain goats, nanny and kid,
regard them from the face of the steeper peak,
a pika, disturbed by their presence, sounds
its shrill alarm, and in the early stillness
the lake's face is dimpled as trout begin to feed.

This year, when they return home, their mother
and wife will, as she always does, ask them
what sort of things they talked about,
and mostly, they will have to admit, they didn't
talk about anything, or else nothing
so important as being there together,
even if while they are there they do talk some.
In truth, it may well be, as she suspects,
that it is this way only because they are men, or becoming
men, this mysterious, baffling masculine silence.

In truth, even knowing she will ask, they don't say much.
Even knowing, among any father and his sons,
there are things in their lives to confront
and make sense of—instruction, confession,
complaint, bewilderment, resentment, all of which

they shouldered into the mountains and will
in three days haul back down again
and carry through their ordinary daily lives still,
the trip to that extent having solved nothing,
though none of them was ever much happier than then.

And yet, something about their nightly rituals—
first lying out on the lake's stone verge
and watching the stars proliferate beyond possibility,
then, the father hardly able to keep his eyes open
and making the first move, each of them drifts
to the margins of camp to brush his teeth,
after which they gather in an open space
and embrace, all three at once, and hold on
what would be in the world they live in
an uncomfortably long time before letting go.

What should their solitude together be called?
How should such a place be measured
against the silence they bring to it
and in which that silence blossoms?
As though it could only grow in this spectacular
and, in truth yet again, humanly uninhabitable spot.
The last day they spent the entire afternoon
watching as a westerly breeze moved a calved
slab of ice from the far side of the lake to their feet,
and when they tried to bring it ashore, it fell apart.

## Cream

It helped to be sixteen and bored a fourth day
deep in the woods, though I like to think it
not just a weariness with trout, mountains, or trees,

but a measure of genius that, having brought back
to his brother and me in camp
the mostly meat-free rib cage of an elk,

my youngest son had also learned that with a mallet of leg bone
he could play on it "Old MacDonald Had a Farm"
and the first five notes of "Sunshine of Your Love."

# But He Did

*1969*

The wind's slow sway held them, and the decade-
old, scavenged lumber tree house, and the tree
it swayed them in held them also, also
the story, the lie, the dead brother one
he borrowed in the graveyard where they met.

And the sway of the tree inside the tree
house allowed the light of the stars to leak
like a slight silver rain all over them—
his arm, her arm, his leg, hers, and music
smoked up from a neighbor's house that summer.

He borrowed the tombstone's good name
and became brother to another, a soldier
lost in the war he himself was bound for,
and borrowed as well the tree house itself
and took her there but did not take her there.

Understand, it was what she wanted too,
even when he told her the truth, which was
that brotherless and drafted he would go,
but he would not go to the war, oh no,
he would not go to the war and die there.

This was how they came to argue of it:
her insistence on the gift of herself
and his insistence he would not accept—
though he very much wanted to—the gift
she would have been and he would not deserve.

It is also how they came to be entwined,
there in the sway of the tree house and wind,
there in the imperceptible motions
of history and the light of the stars,
where he swore he would never lie again.

# Beautiful Country

They had five cigarettes going. Also a joint
        and a foot-and-a-half-high hookah brimmed
with cannabis above and 3.2 beer below.
        A pale blue smaze hung against the high ceiling.
The six who lived there were lotused around
        four unfolded pages of the *San Antonio Express-
News*, stemming and seeding several resinous pounds of pot,
        three of them still in uniform, fatigues at least,
just back from a day at "Special Training Detachment,"
        or as it was emblazoned on their helmet liners
"STD" (a sequence of letters not having, in 1971,
        the resonance or implication they have today).
It was a holding company for the hopeless
        and the hopeful. American soldiers, that is, such as they were.
Also in uniform, person number seven. Call him Sergeant Blinks.
        He'd lost an eye in Vietnam, and he was
their dealer, their source, and he liked them more
        than seemed reasonable or right and promised them
each a free nickel bag for their custodial work.
        And even as they worked, he was strapped off and shooting up
with one of the good sterile syringes
        they'd copped from Central Medical Supply.
That was why he liked them, they figured.
        Come home a junkie, he seemed happy
to be here, since they were to have been medics
        and had stolen those syringes long before
Porter developed the bed-wetting problem and Denton
        and Spiegel decided they were queers (gay, in those days,
meaning only excessively happy), and before the rest of them
        pleaded not merely ordinary fear

but conscientious objection. They said they meant it, in other words,
  even as they wondered how killing Nixon could be anything but right.
When they could talk at all they had those kinds of conversations.
  They thought about what was wrong and more wrong.
Blinks sat in the room's only chair, spike withdrawn now,
  head lolled off to the side, a kind of fractured baleen
of spittle lip to lip across his open mouth.
  The pot was so sticky they paused now and then
to work the goo of it up and off each digit, and rolled it
  into black boluses they dropped in a communal coffee cup—
finger hash, it was called, and they couldn't take their eyes off it,
  redolent, drop deadly, and very much desired.
It would be, at the end of their stem-and-seed-parsing,
  what Sergeant Blinks offered in exchange for his lark:
if he could skin-pop them all with a drop or two of his horse
  in the backs of their six left and mostly white hands, it was theirs.
A long pause then. How bad could it be? they wondered.
  Meaning how good. Meaning they wanted what they wanted
and didn't want what they might come to want more
  or too much of, though what was too much
and what did they really want, after all?
  Well, they wanted that cup of finger hash
enough that no one said no, so happily
  Blinks rigged up five new times: syringes
from the dozens in the stolen box,
  a couple cc's from the bent-back cooking spoon,
and then, in between each of the four metacarpal ridges
  across the backs of their newly brave and unheroic hands,
he eased—so gently, so skillfully—the needle's slender bevel
  just under the skin and made a series of blisters there,

wens, tear-shaped sebaceous cysts of the same stuff
       he had not long before plunged a pistonful of into his vein.
As per his instructions, they flexed their fists
       and slapped the dabbled backs of their hands
with their undabbled others, and felt come rushing up their arms
       a kind of other-coming, overcoming smolder.
Wilson, the one black man among them, studied his biceps
       and said again and again, *Hot fudge, hot fudge.*
It was like entering a large perfect mouth,
       a kind of woman-wetness they were up to their shoulders in,
their necks and ears, until there wasn't anything to say
       and even if there had been no mechanism by which to say it.
But it didn't last long, and as far as they would ever know, none of them
       did it again. And Blinks left them their nickel bags and the sticky stuff,
and Spiegel boiled up the stems and made iced tea from the water.
       They were so wrecked they forgot to eat and sat
on the sun-busted front porch for hours, watching swallows cruise for moths.
       They even stood to salute at sundown and faced up the block
to the base's back gate at Taps,
       and for some reason this was not at all ironic.
Tra-la they would not kill, alas, they would not die.
       They couldn't see the base flag going down,
but the gloaming coming on from the east
       promised another day when everything would be better.
There were bats coming out, hunting.
       America, someone said. Beautiful country.
And it was.

## Hailstorm in the Mountains

You can hear it coming, a storm like this,
        the kind of atmospheric hum you stop
everything to listen for, to hear through,

and by the time you understand its noise
        you can see it too, a stalactite fog,
a warp of ice the green world is weft of.

Only this time you simply let it come:
        no hunting for shelter these last seconds,
there being, after all, nowhere to hide—

no tarp, no poncho, no blanket, no hat.
        Nothing but your man's two hands,
and even those, before the shawl of ice

drapes itself over you, you extend,
        not to catch the stones but to see them travel
up the long, warm distances of your arms.

# Finding a Bible in an Abandoned Cabin

Under dust plush as a moth's wing,
the book's leather cover still darkly shone,
and everywhere else but this spot was sodden
beneath the roof's unraveling shingles.
There was that back-of-the-neck lick of chill,
and then, from my index finger, the book

opened like a blasted bird. In its box
of familiar and miraculous inks,
a construction of filaments and dust,
thoroughfares of worms, and a silage
of silverfish husks: in the autumn light,
eight hundred pages of perfect wordless lace.

# Exxon

Behold the amazing artificial arm, a machine
eerily similar to the arm it replaced, machined
to exacting *tolerances*, as its engineers say,
to "the limits of allowable error."
Think of the hand in the glove, the piston
in the cylinder, the cartridge in the chamber
of an arm: a weapon, that is, a firearm,
to say it more primitively, more exactingly,

more ceremonially, and with more appropriate awe.
Behold then the arm from which fire comes, the hand
of a god hurling lightning. Behold the digital trigger, tick of
the finger on the hand separated from its body by the bomb
at the police station, the rifle smoking
just beyond it, as though it might yet shoot again,
the digital tick of the bomb's timer also disembodied now.

Study the artificial arm, its array of hex-
head setscrews, its titanium armatures and axes,
its silicone skins from light pink to dark brown.
Here is this, from the company's catalog: "The upper
and lower forearm tubes are secured
to a four-position, manually locked elbow mechanism."
And this, from God himself, having slain the man's family,
saying to Job, *Or hast thou an arm like God?*

And, *Wilt thou also disannul my judgment?*
*Wilt thou condemn me, that thou mayest be righteous?*
The nerve, and the lack. Beyond the limits of allowable error,

beyond the art of it, the story of Job, the trajectory
of narrative, the flight of the bearings and nails,
the improvised explosive device; beyond war itself, that honored
aesthetic ever-present evil alive and vile in the story
that is a lie about the truth and the truth, great engineer

help us, of the lie. Consider the ongoing
problem of tactile sensitivity, the elusiveness
of feeling, those of us otherwise untouched touched
for several dollars a gallon. And see the soldier in parade dress
easing with his other, non-silicone fingers a credit card into
and removing it rapidly from the slot
in the pump, and entering through its portal
the world of disembodied money

and the exacting tolerances of the world banking
system: behold this soldier, and know of his doubts
about the surrendering of arms, which is to say not only
the ambiguous tolerances of the Second Amendment
but the limb abandoned in Baghdad;
the soldier who has entered also into the system
of government surveillance—the porn sites,
the blogs, the maimed-in-the-line-of-duty

collectorates, the whiskeys and women, the rehabilitations.
See the soldier who nods and whose left
intact hand extended to your extended right one
confuses you an instant, but who nods again
to relieve you in your awkwardness. And behold them,

your untouched touched hands, as he nestles his man-made
right one over both of yours on his left, feeling,
between his old self and his new, a responsible citizen.

# Do Not Go

My father hated loving dogs, since they did so shed,
and messed, chewed, and barked, et cetera too.
Fried chicken neither he did not care for,
it being "hard to eat," or rather
hard to clean up from. He disapproved of that.
Watermelon, he believed, should with a plate and fork be et.

But lo, he can no longer wash his own car and I cry truly,
so many miles away I cannot wash the thing for him,
though the air cleaner from it even today I would
for a plate underneath a watermelon slab
use and fear of foreign substances not in the least.

But why is it no longer, as in the past, a foreign car, I ask you?
I would ask him, but he would agree and seek
therefore a new one, appropriately foreign,
that, alas, at his advanced age, in his condition,
he could not, alas, drive, alas. Alas,

the long-haired lass I kept undressing night after night
in his backseat years of summer nights ago
like some beautiful sweaty dog shed
so many of her long, long hairs he asked me
was she bald, the poor girl? And I said oh yes, she was,

and he thought, I think, I was just being smart.
But no, I am still very lucky. And all through those years
he kept changing the cars everyone else in the family drove
but him for no reason the rest of us could see
except for maybe dog and girl hair

and some need not the least, we didn't think, acquisitive,
though cars, it seems, are an acquired taste after all, one which
I have not myself developed. If the motherfucker just goes, great.
Though not him, oh no, not my mother's lover of cars,
not my father, who since they so shed, hates loving dogs still.

## What the Night Horse Runs From

The horse runs around the pasture at night for
or from what but its own astonishing tail,
a pennant, a wind-thing it never seems to notice or
simply cannot get away from after dark. Sail

of hair driving it, or something I can't say?
Only by star- or moonlight do I think I see it,
behind the tail's black, the horse's mahogany bay.
Still, as that something flashes by, I wish I could be it.

# Hourglass

Of his collection, an old man said, "So much time
standing still unless upended."
Who has never wanted to turn around its passage?
The hour of love, the shudder at the edge
of the first kiss, the misstep and fall, the slip
that told too much of the momentary truth.

When Jace was four, he lay on his back
rotating minute by minute the three-minute
timer from a child's game, and asked
"Do you know what this is, Daddy?" Then he told me
without looking away: "Time sugar."
The end of such a sweetness is also an ache.

Regarding the metaphor for her figure,
I swear it was the vehicle that stopped time
and again too short: you could spend a year
loving the full swells out of and into which the spill
seemed minutely to cipher her voluptuousness,
though it was the middle made it all of a piece.

Old gnomon of the sundial, a shepherd's tally stick, the water
clock's drip-drop prefiguring the pendulum's tock,
a day cloven into twelves sixty by sixty ticks around.
Or the stuff of glass subsiding in a glass
of such a shape, all I want to do, as time keeps passing,
is to watch it go by.

## Ashtray in the Snow

If I had been more careful last December,
I'd have stowed the pair of chairs and the stump
table under the studio, so that

today, as spring snow melts off the porch,
I would not see this faceted glass thing
emerge like a reef of ice from the white sea,

nor, for that matter, the great fractured mast
of last year's final cigar, lying athwart
a broken shard, its nub of ash a raven.

# A Rumor of Bears

The truck's heater gasped a damp, phantom dog
into the cab, redolent of rain-soaked wool.
Its choke and vent was anything but warm.

The day had faded dull—gray sun, gray rain.
Even the slim college girls walking by
wore fat coats the colors of wildebeests,

and the aging dour professors limping
among them were plainly no threat at all.
I should have known it would be like this, come

as I had from the bears, having hoisted,
just after her blood draw, the knocked-out sow
up onto a low rickety gurney.

Three other men and I took coarse fistfuls
of grizzly hair, rolled her down a hall
to a cinderblock hibernaculum,

and placed her upright on her great bear gut,
so that she might sleep silent until spring.
After that, the tedium of roads too

often seen, nullity of autumn fields,
vast dullard blandness of the same way home.
But when I stepped up onto the front porch,

the black cat's back arched, and the snagged nuthatch fell
from her jaws and flew unsteadily off.
"Hey, Lily," I said, but she hissed and skipped up

the nearest tree, then glared back down at me and yowled.
She kept it up even when I walked inside,
where the young dog, a pup almost, rolled over,

wet herself, and slunk off to another room.
As for the old dog, her tail began its thump-thumping
at my voice, that low familiar verity

she knew, even in her diminished state—
almost blind, incapable of running—
as everything right and true, all things safe.

"It's me, Violet," I said. "It's me, girl."
That's when I smelled my hands for the first time.
They were ripe: pure bear feculence and musk,

swampy crotch-lands and scrotal dews,
flowers of flesh and blood, a rank bouquet.
I knelt down close, and for just that moment

feared the reek of me might kill her all by itself.
Her eyes narrowed, the loose whitened cheek flaps
drew back toward a snarl, she stiffened and sniffed,

then took in a thing she had never smelled
the shape of before. "It's just me," I said
again, and my hand against the black rose

of her durable, most sensitive nose
made her flinch and retreat as I sat,
a man-whiff of mouth-tastes festered through sleep,

all the tart pungencies of fly-blown eyes;
of peristalsis, lanolin, and gristle—
she could not take her snout away from me.

Understand, I had never been a man,
an ordinary, plain man, to this dog.
There was no fearsome where, there was nothing

she would not have faced, or welcomed, with me,
which is why she fought her way to her feet
and why I stood with her and walked to the door.

She was ready. She could smell the clawed thing
perched mewling in the tree, and its fear too.
She could smell a high fence and concrete, a thousand

olfactory miles unrun, the meat cache
and the scum, even some other creature's vision—
spring beauties, yellow bells, bear feasts of bulbs and grubs.

Slowly, slowly, she traced a path back to the truck,
useless ears pricked up and constantly searching,
smelling what, I wondered, if not joy—

all the wild, lithe come-hithers of carrion,
of tallow and gut, the lure of fine, sweet death.
Though in fact the old dog is dead now too,

gone within a week of that once-drab Monday,
when I came to her, superfluous
with meaningful stinks, explosively new,

and she rose and lead me into the woods,
having smelled on my man's hands a rumor
of bears, the scent of a vanishing world.

# American Fear

*"Such as we were we gave ourselves outright."*
—Robert Frost

What it is is a company selling "clothing
            for the disaffected youth culture,"
T-shirts and sweatshirts, mostly black,
            someone's marketing vision for a new world,
a twenty-first-century Henry ("You can have
            any color you want so long as it's black") Ford,
that old-time anti-Semite, his once nearly bankrupt
            namesake corporation supplanted by this other.

A button on the Web site reads "Ready to Order Fear,"
            but everywhere you look it's free: fear of wolves,
bulls, and bears; fear of the sun, fear of that one
            or this one, fear that all it takes is one. Storm fear,
house fear, fear of frost. Fear of gravity is barophobia.
            But there's also Cape Fear, Camp Fear,
and Fear Mountain: you can visit those. There's fear
            of God, fear of the odd; fear of night, fear of air.

Fear of hair is chaetophobia. Eleutherophobia's fear of freedom.
            There's *First Encounter Assault Recon*,
"a survival horror first-person shooter developed
            by Monolith Productions and published by Vivendi,"
a video game, a generation's modus vivendi, a way of living
            in which we agree to disagree violently.
Ephebiphobia is the fear of teenagers; melanophobia,
            fear of the color black; caligynephobia,

fear of beautiful women; and anthrophobia, fear
            of flowers. You can spend hours on a list like this.

Pantophobia is the fear of everything. After
              230-odd years the republic crawls
through its slow-motion youth, democracy requiring not
              only equality but a vast sameness many fear,
as some fear guns and others fear their guns
              will be taken away, their beautiful guns,

poetry in them, shining assemblages of articulate parts
              in which ammo is the main idea. Consider the idea
that a thing can be beyond perfection, as in a more perfect
              union, as in the sky and its endlessness
—astrophobia, that's called: the fear of stars
              and celestial space. As for fear of oblivion,
there is no word for it. Come home late, Robert Frost
              rattled the key in the lock and left the door open

until a light was on, a way of allowing what was inside out.
              Later, on his farmhouse porch, Frost trembling,
frightened of the dark, a shotgun in his hands. He thought
              he could talk Khrushchev into nuclear disarmament
(nucleomituphobia, bomb fear) and sulked because
              JFK didn't call him back. The fear of poetry
is metrophobia, and melophobes fear music, cringing
              at the ballgame through "God Bless America."

Regarding the disaffected, the *OED* suggests they lack
              first of all affection. Put that with logophobia,
the fear of words, and philophobia, the fear of love.
              Parthenophobia is the fear of virgin girls. WTF

is Internet slang and the initials of the World Taekwondo
        Federation, member of the International Olympic Committee.
Why is there no word for the fear of committees,
        which are so much to be feared? Fear of Germany

is teutophobia. Vestiphobia is the fear of clothing.
        The fear of flags is vexiphobia. On American Fear's
logo, you can find the flag's stripes resembling a bar code.
        Gringophobia is the fear of Americans, the ones
who fear America ends far north of Tierra del Fuego.
        Fear of a white god is leukotheophobia. A snowclone
is a "cliché or phrasal template, multiuse, customizable,
        instantly recognizable, timeworn, and open

to an array of variants"—as in, *What Would Henry Ford Do?*
        American Fear's best-selling design:
a mandible-less skull enwreathed by bullets, bunting,
        and feathers, on a base of fifties-befinned bombs.
There is no word for the fear of growing up,
        though gerascophobia is the fear
of growing old, and old men fear not
        how others might read them by their clothes.

Kings wear robes and senators wear suits. The word *senator*
        comes from the Latin *senex*, meaning "old man,"
and gerontophobia is the fear of old people.
        Chronophobia is the fear of time.
Some old men do not wear T-shirts,
        because putting one on can be exhausting

and taking it off worse. Imagine fearing a shirt.

    Why is there a word like *bathysiderodromophobia*?

Subways are beautiful in their tunnels and troughs,

    their soiled, palatial stations. "Go in fear of abstractions,"

Pound said. He suffered not from metrophobia,

    but from madness. "To fear" in Italian is *temere.*

"What thou lovest well remains, the rest is dross,"

    wrote Pound. "Better to go down dignified

with boughten friendship at your side than none at all,"

    wrote Frost. He had a lover's quarrel with the world.

Among American Fear's other shirt designs, one called

    "Your Pretty Death Bed," a young woman,

her wrists slashed, looking asleep and covered

    by the Stars and Stripes. There is no word

for the fear our daughters will commit suicide

    beneath a patriotic blanket. Robert Frost's son, Carol,

shot himself with a deer rifle on October 9, 1940.

    "I took the wrong way with him," wrote Frost,

who would outlive all but two of his six children.

    A citizen opposes the reintroduction of gray wolves

to the American wilderness, because they are Canadian,

    as though they might harbor within their genes

a disinclination for revolution and a soft spot

    for the queen. Freddie Mercury was a gay British genius,

and homophobic sports teams all across the nation sing his

    "We Are the Champions." He's number 50

among the 100 Greatest Britons, four slots ahead
        of George Harrison, twelve ahead of Jane Austen,
and a whopping twenty-three in front of Geoffrey Chaucer.
        Ronald Reagan is number one on the American list.
The only poet in the top twenty-five is Muhammad Ali,
        who comes in just above Rosa Parks but well behind
Elvis, whose pelvis was censored from the television screen.
        No word for the fear of free speech,

but a man was not allowed to board a flight at JFK
        because his T-shirt, in Arabic and English, read,
"We will not be silent." American Fear's shirts
        will not alarm the Transportation Security Administration,
also called the TSA. The fear of silence is sedatephobia.
        The TSA is also the Tourette Syndrome Association,
and based on Boswell's descriptions it is theorized
        that Samuel Johnson suffered from the malady,

making frequent odd grunts and muttering
        under his breath "too, too, too," meaning also
and yes and more, meaning many,
        meaning he meant to know all the words,
and the problem with all is everything. All men, all words,
        all fears. This beautiful, fearful,
and fearsome country, such as it is,
        such as it might yet, someday, become.

# Night Walk

Despite the moonlessness, a glow still lives
in the lighter stones, yonder a great seam
of quartz beams stars back at the stars.
The night-walking habit he cannot shake,
and shunning headlamp or flashlight he goes slow.
He knows the way through the woods well, sometimes
waits a spell, took a hard fall once it was hard
to get up from, to giddyup again through a dark like that,

or like this one is, under the interrogations of an owl.
He heard an owl die once, bird he had to go back
next day in sunlight to be certain of, and sure enough,
the rabbit it had taken stiff, back broke, untouched
on the fallen snag the owl had taken it to, behind which the bobcat
happened to be. He'd heard some wing-silence shaken,
deathly hard, a feather tear, *sproing* and bone-pop.
How it is he came to have an owl skull and claws.

Saw against a fender a man's shadow take from behind
a woman's once, heard her bleat, his rut-grunt.
Saw them by dome-glow and music dress, ruby lights
of their driving back down the mountain road
what left him blind. And what has blinded him otherwise?
Fog, Perseid chunks, space junk, *whump* of deer
upleaping out of brush, his own warm house aglow.

And he wants a cape almost, wants lampblack cheekbones,
wants to go Rathboning, Lugosified, a child of god
nocturnal and bewinged if only in the brain.
Wants moonlessness, wants to slither close enough

to love cars and rabbit disembowelments
he can hear in the sounds of them each slit and gush;
wants to rush into the dark, into the hundred
undiscovered shades of black and live there.

But does not. Always comes back, always.
Even wholly lightless his house
emits a vaporous, unearthly glow.
The long hall to the bedroom shines
invisibly, the waters of the shower bathe
the shape of him with blindness, and the bed
dark as a grave welcomes him in.
And he walks in his sleep through a forest

enleaved with the wings of ravens, black
as the belly of the mountain's deepest stone.
Stars like coal darkly shimmer and the moon
unshines, an amulet of ink from which he extracts
the few elemental words for all he still sees—
obsidian, adamantine, anthracite, tar.
Smoke from his fire drifts liquid as a river,
the night's living blood he moves through.

# Soap

When I consider the worn, petal-scented bar of soap
my lover inadvertently left in the deep woods,
alongside the river we camped by for a week,

I think first of watching her bathe there,
how I waited with her towel in the sun, her clean clothes
warming on the radiant stones.

Then I think of a man not unlike myself finding it,
a pink and botanical soap, in a perfectly scooped dish
on the back of a large, water-polished rock.

He senses her in the curve and slope
of its undoing at her skin, and holding it
to his lips he takes in some faint but vivid

scent of her, stepping clean into her towel and my arms,
which now are his, and who then, unable to help himself,
offers the soap's pale astringent underside a kiss.

## What Is Yellow About the Yellow Pine?

Not the wood, which is white-to-beige-to-red,
nor the bark, nor the cones, not even the dying needles
gone brown directly from green:

what is yellow is the air around them
in spring, and the wind-shadow cast from west to east,
as everything also on the face of the earth

within a mile of a forest of them is washed
by their pollen, paler and purer than saffron.
Everything plucked up from the ground

is likewise silhouetted there, a darkened absence.
Even those of us who sleep
on the other side of screens,

through which passes all night long
their silent, seemingly weightless golden breath:
we rise in the morning and see the sun

as it gleams around the shining rim
of where we lay our individual darknesses down,
the upper halves of us dusted, yellow, shining.

## None Shall Sleep

The pang and clangor of pitch dense wood
in the stove and the odd, almost-syncopated
pops of studs, joists, and rafters as they warm;

coyote howls and the hard wind that brings
and takes them away; the chuffs and slumps
as snow pods slip from limbs and thunder

onto the roof; the hourly scrape as three feet
of accumulation up there sloughs gradually loose—
it will give way all at once when it is forgotten;

the nervousness of prey in the vanished silence
of the night. Though when the pitch is gone
and the fire goes quiet as a candle; when

walls and floor and ceiling stand and stretch
to their extent; when the coyotes move off
to hunt and the wind subsides, and the falling

snow resumes its vertical imperative; when
the trees take up their noble stillnesses
and the roof's heavy snow load rests

on the ground; when the deer and elk can hear
again each needle sway and cold twig subsidence.
What is the name of a silence that deep?

## After a Rainstorm

Because I have come to the fence at night,
the horses arrive also from their ancient stable.
They let me stroke their long faces, and I note
in the light of the now-emerging moon

how they, a Morgan and a Quarter, have been
by shake-guttered raindrops
spotted around their rumps and thus made
Appaloosas, the ancestral horses of this place.

Maybe because it is night, they are nervous,
or maybe because they too sense
what they have become, they seem
to be waiting for me to say something

to whatever ancient spirits might still abide here,
that they might awaken from this strange dream,
in which there are fences and stables and a man
who doesn't know a single word they understand.

## Old Bucket

The bottom was an unaxled wheel of oak
circumferenced by a kerf a thumb knuckle wide.
Into this gap seated the staves' blunt ends,
all held in place by the pair of iron rings—
a top one with tangs for the carrying bail
and another at the waist for tension.

But this old bucket had been parts and rubble,
a cardboard box of clatters and clanks
the wood of which I soaked all night in a tub
and fitted together in a yoke of twine
before hammering over it all the upside-down top ring,
followed by the bottom one, to rebuild it.

But why? Since it continually weeps at least,
or worse, its hand-coopered slats
no longer flush or plumb, no matter how long
I let the sunken thing also soak reassembled.
Though I suppose that's what might have saved it
all its long, useless years,

that it always leaked a little, which caused it
to be consigned first to the barn, then a cellar,
where before it was found it fell apart.
Still, the dog drinks from it, and it looks good
on the porch there, where she laps, and its leak falls
to feed, drop by drop, the red climbing rose.

## Cemetery Moles

Most are not blind, but still,
might the concrete burial vaults
be perceived before a tunnel
comes to such a sudden hard naught?

Though I notice their mounds mostly
down here with the old stones, last row—
those graves that are not only
vaultless but with a wooden casket too.

And the stories from the sexton?
A filled tooth on a hill whitely shining,
and a mole in a trap one early June,
around its neck a wedding ring.

## Full Moon and Horse

How first the mane's errant hairs crystallize
darkly into shapes, into loops and wires.
How all the shed tail shreds glimmer blackly
on the fence, and how his breaths ghost outward,
and the grasses he'd cropped the tops of crisp
beneath the coming frost, how he nickers
and snorts. How he stamps a hind hoof and stops
his chewing as the pasture around him
sinks into darkness, and how the barn beckons
and the wind shifts the weather vane to west
in a rusty familiar screech. How night
shifts to the new shadows everywhere.
How the slope of his long black back glistens.
How for half a minute the huge moon sits him
rider-like and bareback before it shrinks
risen to the night-light he knows it as, and how
by walking with him you can keep it there
almost, as though he were taking its glow
for its own safekeeping into the stall
his chin over years has worn the rails of
to a smoothness he is comforted by.
How he works his neck and ear on a post.
How the ancient shakes dispense the moonlight
in a sky beneath the sky, full of stars.
How he sleeps standing. How he rests each leg
in turn, how his dreams rumble, how he breathes
and shivers in his skin, how the sweet hay
smells tincture the leather odor of tack.
How the moon's paled light slides east to west
along the clean-swept hard-trodden dirt floor,

how in a few hours more it will enter
the unshuttered barn window behind him
and find its silver memory in what sweat
the sun brought from his hide the day before.
How the sun will come again in such gloom
as will rouse him, as it always does,
to enter a day made completely new—
even the old circumnavigations
reinvented along the trapezoidal shape
the fence encloses, which he will run.
And how he will run, how that run will come
from the long night he stood through, sound asleep,
once you've left the barn's deep semidarkness
and walked among the droppings-salted dewy
grass hummocks to the gate, and let yourself out,
taking all the night's rest of it on faith.

## Which Last

In the thicket just west of my shack,
under the heaviest of canopied pines,

every day, all winter long, two does recline
and rest, and sometimes when I look

from the window their eyes are closed,
but still they go on chewing whatever

snowbound vegetation they've uncovered—
or just their sad, inadequate cuds, I suppose.

As I suppose my daily apple also
is due to them. I've been a little slow to learn

not to throw the core and make them run,
but to toss it gently between us, like so,

then go inside and watch through the glass,
to see which is the lucky first one to it, which last.

## A Lock of Her Hair

As a hoodoo-voodoo, get-you-back-to-me tool,
this hank's thankless task is vast,
a head-down-to-the-ground impossibility, possibly,
since what I'm thinking of is your toe pad pinknesses too,
your soup hots and round-and-rounds, the fine
and perfect poundage of you on my paws, the very cause
and problem I moan for and bemoan
the absence of. For Love, above the head
this reddish coil once lavishly wore, there's an air so far away
it's sad for me to even think the same sun's rays play
where it was and do to you what I would do
if I were there or you were here. Still, some thrills
remembered do resemble thrills, one hopes, and the ropes
of it that gently fell around me bound me so well
no hell of miles can defile this dream I dream. I mean
the anyway DNA I can find of you. I mean the home
of bones and blood that holds the whole of you
and which this fizzed-up missive means to conjure, missy,
my world in a curl, girl, this man oh man half man I am
when you're gone.

## Available Light

And what would I do with another picture
            of her nude? The ones I have I show to no one,
                        not even her anymore, for fear she might
want them back, or worse. But the one
            I regret not taking most was that hot
                        summer night I rose for a drink of water,
not even noticing at first I was alone,
            until, in the hallway of the too-small house
                        we lived in then, I saw her fully extended
on our son's bed. He had a summer cold
            and a little lifelong jones for the breast.
                        He was two, almost. He'd been fussy from the heat,
so she went to him there, and then there
            she was too, sleeping—and all her long back, head to heel.
                        In my half-wakefulness I stood, ciphering
such a photograph's mechanics: tripod, cable release,
            the long moon- and night-lighted, sepia-toned exposure. . . .
                        When I told her years later how close I'd come,
she said I should have, it would have been fine,
            and there lies the source of my regret: her late permission.
                        Though I think of it now only as I slip the others
from the safe place they're hidden in,
            six in all: three along a mountain river;
                        one in a galvanized tub at the hot springs;
another, fishing from the shore of a mountain lake, in sunglasses—
            and then the absent one, framed by the doorway:
                        on the nearest edge of a twin bed,
a stuffed bear looking on from the cast-off sheets,
            the rasping boy out of sight on the other side of her,
                        and a particular sheen on her skin, as if

she'd been basted or entirely, relentlessly kissed,
      even the bottoms of her slender, delectable feet
    aglow.

# Campfire

*from the journals of D. D. Pye (1871–1890)*

For the twigs, being dry and loosely stacked, burned
swiftly, and the kindling, being hewn from a long-standing larch snag,
was also ideally seasoned and crackled brightly into flames.
Then the first small log splits likewise ignited, and I rested there
on my rock, the ever-darkening night cooling the back of my neck
as my face flushed with the glow and heat of the fire.

This was when I chanced to see an ant emerge
from a hole in the smooth bark side of the last length of wood
I had offered to the flames. Although his situation, surely, could not
have been more dire, he seemed calm in his side-to-side explorations
of the log, scurrying away from an edge only once
when a smoke cloud wafted its acrid breath in his face.

By way of experiment, I laid a long slender branch
from the stones of the fire ring to the opposite end of what was both
his potential death-plank and temporary salvation, calculating that,
if resourcefulness and survival ticked as saliently in his jet encasement
as it did within my own skin, he would find this route
to safety eventually. Which he did, but as his bad luck would have it,

from deep within the log he'd perhaps long called home, a pitch pocket,
having reached a temperature from which its brew could no longer expand,
blew with no more than a campfire pop, hardly even a report,
but hard enough to shake from their flaming superstructures
both the log and the bridge I had provided into the flames,
taking the ant as well, whom by now I had in my lonesomeness

become exceedingly glad for, although he was gone in an instant
in the seethe of those coals. This was the point at which I became aware

first of the excessive heat upon my face, so rapt had I been
at my watching, and then, looking up toward the coolness of the night,
aware also of an abundance of stars beyond any man's ability
to reason, let alone cipher or bear, let alone be alone beneath.

# Bergschrund

It's the space between the mountain's face
and the glacier's uphill wall. And we were small there.
I pulled a soggy boot up from the muck and stepped blind
into a slickrock chute and skidded on my back
twenty feet into the icy underspace the summer's melting had made.
Stones the size of small cars glowered down from their settings.
My hiking partner, the one who'd wanted to see
the bergschrund in the first place, collapsed in laughter.
We were headed down, after all, back to camp, and based on
the distant light come up from the bottom, I believe I could have
slithered all the way down that way and, being young, probably
should have, probably should have understood
of all the places we wanted to believe we were the first men
to have stood in, this, in the timelessness of its ice, was likeliest.
I should have slithered around to my belly, as I did,
and crawled not up but down, and yelled upward under
the rounded facets of the glacier's gut, *I'm going this way.*
But I didn't do it, my biggest regret now,
since I'm almost sixty, and in the last ten years
of the more than thirty since that day, the glacier's ancient waters,
under the otherwise unchanged face of the mountain, are gone.

# Memoir

The odious travails, the nascent lusts,
that blue blade of betrayal I cut myself so badly on.
So much schooling, and for what?
This pluperfect curveball? These theoretical
martinis? Even the music of the spheres was flat
in those days, the bowling ball of one's fate

careering along for years, promise leaking
from its finger holes. Then I came to a fork,
one of those top-end knockoff
stainless steel three-tine jobs,
a little meat-gaff bean shanking mashed potato trowel.
The duchess fed me with it, marshmallows

warmed in her décolletage. Therefore I volunteered.
The battles grievous, the radio reception
questionable, the long industrial pipeline
in the breeding of ever-tinier dogs. In my foxhole
each night I composed the canticles of my losses:
a cousin, a chiropractor, a loaf of bread, a cow.

The shadows of admirals darkened my past,
consulates and missionaries, my supermodel mother,
my father, though deaf, recording the cello suites
of Bach on a Jew's harp. My ugly twin brother,
the acute if whiskery seductiveness of my sister.
As for the children, nothing is too good for them.

## "Little Prick"

*an Englishman in Austin, Texas, March 2006*

The problem with calling our leader a bugger,
she insisted, was her particular fondness
for buggerers, and by implication, what buggery
those buggerers did, not to mention Her Blondeness's
own predilections. The wink said what her
words half did, as did her crossed eyes and muggery.

That was just months ago, and he can't remember
all the epithets, scurrilous and tasty, spewing
from her lips and concerning the great leader's member,
its length and girth piss-poor and never doing;
a sort of thing about his thing, a verbal emasculation
he felt himself rise to, for the good of her nation.

Though in the end she was chagrined
also by him, who could not—even with the promise
of such rewards as she had just implied,
even with her wayward republic itself in the balance—
deliver with wit. Though if you had said what did not happen
was also the president's fault, neither would have denied it.

## All Souls

It's late in the season, but still I leave the zucchini
to grow inedibly large, thinking
elongated green jack-o'-lanterns
or the county fair's generous blue ribbon.

Even after the invasion of the squash beetles—
stalks sucked dry, the vast desiccate hands
of the leaves doilied over the fruits' broad flanks—
they seem to go on growing.

This one I call Lenny. Imagine him,
burning from within, massively bottomed,
stooge-betopped, tiny dim eyes high in his skull,
and over his crooked mouth, a mustache of flame.

# Night Music

Full moon and wide forest trail make the headphones possible.
He need not walk by ear but is allowed all the way
to nowhere in particular and back Bach's Brandenburg
concerti, music as lavish and intricate as the pine needle
lacework shadowed along the ground he walks.

What shuffles and skitters, what hoof thumps running
away as he passes, he does not hear, but hears instead
the basso continuo and violins; what inquiries of owl
and crescendo of coyotes he also does not hear, but hears
instead an oboe and French horns calling in his ears.

He fears, therefore, nothing, and allows the day's
wet fallen snow to rumble soundless under his boots
as he walks a mile, and then more, from home.
As many as the stars, the notes of Bach's music,
as many as the Brandenburg's movements, the eyes

he's seen, seeing him pass like a kind of god,
which the margrave of Brandenburg, Bach's benefactor,
was also not, having insufficient musicians to perform
the concerti, and who therefore left the full score unplayed
in his library, until it was sold, upon the margrave's death,

in 1734, for twenty-four groschen, twenty-four small
silver coins, which end-to-end would barely extend
a quarter the width of the trail our man, deaf to the woods
and the mountain night, walks and even, eventually,
begins to gesture his way down, up, and over, conducting

with his blunt, mittened hands the virtuoso stars,
an orchestra of light and forest and snow, through which
he walks a mile or more from home, and returns,
so that at the end of concerto number six, we see him bowing
and shaking the hand of the first violinist, the wind.

# Duff

Under the deep needle thatch
more needles, and under those,
shanks of needles and darkly thinning hunks,
the ghost bones of had-been needles.
A slurry of carapace and pupal shale,
a billion desiccate curds, pellet and turd,
and the vast imponderable leavings
I love to scratch through, a kind of subcontinent,
a wilderness domesticated by rot,
in which, every now and then, I unearth
and turn up once again to the sun
something that my eyes might cherish
more than the suckling mouths of microbes do—
this delicate white arch, for instance, the mandible of a vole;
this mummified pinfeather stub, its boutonniere
of down like the gray wiry hair in a god's ear;
or strangest of all, this odd isosceles triangle
made of interlocked paper clips and rust.
I dangle it on an autumn bare syringa twig
where a junco might find it and by any bird's standards
build with it a superior nest.

## They Are Bidden

Whose kids they were I cannot imagine,
the ones who crucified a cat to this tree.
Three of them, I'd guess, given what recoil and thrash
survival would have packed inside the blaze of wrath
and desperation any cat would be, not just this one.
Unless they'd brained it first, a rap to the skull
with this very shanked-off barkless heft of limb I hold.
Or unless it was dead already, and everything here then
the kind of flirtatious, demonic window-dressing
might appeal to a certain sort of boy
and his minions, the little ones who love
and do as they are bidden and dream
of being the one who bids.

When I was a kid I was enraged
at the assumption, always, that whatever ill
was done was done by a boy, though by a boy
it almost always was done, it's true. And the thing
about a girl who would do such a thing
is that there isn't any other thing she might not do,
even with a boy, if a boy could also be convinced,
and what boy I ever knew could not be.
Of course, I would never have done such a thing as this,
or at least I am glad no one ever convinced me to.
It is hard, in the face of the cat, to face
the cat. I have no tool to pry loose the heavy nails,
so that wondering who might have driven them

and what they said as they hammered
allows me—for all the detail I might yet include,

as I slide the aforementioned limb stob
behind the stiffened corpse and lever it loose—to think
not of the bones therein nor the raven-savored gone
eyes of it, but rather of the eyes of whoever it was
bartered his baby soul to be a part of this
and what for. In the interests of felinity, I choose
to believe it was dead already when they did it,
whoever they were I cannot imagine even as I do.
Afterward there would have been words to try out
and the sweet shivering chill of damnation,
when one said to the other, Now you can hold my hand.

## Such Giants

You could pin the kitchen match
against the striker patch of its box
and flick it, and thereby send it flying
with its flame toward the forsaken
green plastic soldier, who stood taking aim
from his puddle of lighter fluid doom.

And we were fond of such ordnance
as we possessed, and eventually gathered
all our armies, his and mine, now
impossible to tell apart, and finding
the lighter fluid insufficient for the lake
such legions required, brought

from the garage a cottage cheese carton
full of lawn mower gas, which, when
at last one of our matches hit the mark,
blew with such force we were each
splattered with our own battalions
and had to stomp the little riflemen out

in the grass and toss them hot potato back
onto the conflagration. The smoke
was acrid and lasted half an hour,
then the mass hardened to a green and blackened disk
in the middle of the sidewalk,
and which he, being even then

some kind of artist, pried up and took home
and hung on the wall of the tree house
from which we plotted the ordinary mayhem
of ordinary boys. That his body
in all these years has never been found
among the patties and lavish soils of Vietnam

perplexed his parents far more
than his death. That his name
took me most of an hour to find
on the Wall, and that the rubbing I made
of it there has been misplaced somewhere
reminds me of how we lay for days

on the tree house boards, noting
the passage of the sun across the sky
through the roof's abundance of holes,
and how now and then a single beam
would light our only item of decor,
that scorched green ovoid on the wall,

a frieze of elbows and rifle stocks, bepebbled
with helmets, one or two faces looking out
exactly as in life, or what passed for it
for them, who'd been, we understood,
the medium in which such giants as us worked.
The great maple swayed under us

some days. Would-be Napoleons, little
danger-yearners, little needers to make
from a kitchen match a bomb. He said
he hated the world, and I, not knowing what else
to do, picked at the burn scab on my chin
relentlessly, hoping for a useful, warning scar.

## At a Cabin in the Woods

The candle lit the room just enough
to render every window a mirror,
and each time he approached one nearer
than he had intended, he felt some touch
of unease come over him, some chill of fear.

Thus, the little cabin shrank around him,
and night drew up to it blacker than before.
His steps on the porch thundered, and the roar
of his pissing was louder than it seemed.
He nearly bolted for the cabin door
when the stars above caught his eyes.

How could so much light leak in and still
he could not see? And what did the coyotes' shrill
songs portend but the silence improvised
by every death's satisfying thrill?
He thought death, not dying, might be a thing
a man could imagine: it seemed a kind of dream.

But how could nothing be a thing that seemed?
How could impossible distances ring
with silence? A star's light heavy as a beam?
He laughed, and laughter filled the meadow up.
How enormous he'd come to be out here,
above him stillness and a satellite's sear.

Outside, he rattled his window self with a tap,
knowing there was no one there.

# Wait

He also finds the wood and steel beautiful,
and the slickness with which all the moving parts
slide open and shut, lifting and lodging
into place the sleek, copper-clad,
steel-jacketed projectile, which, weighing less
than half an ounce, will cover, once

the trigger is pulled, the eighty yards to the doe
in the time it would take him to blink.
He aligns the crosshairs of the scope
just behind her right shoulder, where the heart
pumps and the lungs, she being absolutely at ease
and grazing, exchange the same mountain air

he also breathes, though he breathes less easily,
since he hopes the single shot will kill her
cleanly and knows, even so, that
should such a clean kill be accomplished, still
he will mourn and be glad simultaneously and will
for the next hour or more be bathed in her blood

and intimate with the then-stilled machinery
of her living—the yards of guts, the probably full
bladder, the buttery liver, and more—nearly all
of which he will leave on the forest floor,
and all of which but the head of her will, he is certain,
be gone within two days, a blessing for the coyotes

and the black and white custodial birds. Even still,
he has not yet squeezed the bullet free but breathes
with her to be free of her, allowing each breath
to elongate, allowing himself to see and to note
how the light snow that has been falling
all morning lands on her shoulders

and on the dry last leaves of the shrubs
just behind her and even, though he does not see it,
on the barrel of the rifle itself, some of which,
from the concussion of the shot, will fall away,
and some, due to the fire that accompanies it,
will melt and refreeze as ice as he works on her: the doe

who had discovered so close to the coming winter
the same patch of long and still green mountain fescue
he himself found some weeks ago on a walk, the same day
he found this other spot as well—sheltered, slightly elevated—
from which the fine grass and all ways to it could be seen, the day
he knew all he'd have to do was wait long enough, as he has.

## Yorick

The big bull moose I call Hamlet mouthed
a wad of ninebark leaves, ruminating
in the way of his kind, but also ours,
having noticed, I noticed, the long-gone
spike buck's skull grinning up at him eating.

That Hamlet then let fly a steaming pile
of fat moose pellets made me wonder some
about the funeral rites of men,
though I also wondered, when Hamlet nudged
the skull's upstanding horn, what it was he felt.

A stob to maybe scratch a long snout on, I thought,
but did he also think, that great bull moose—
who never stopped chewing, who took a shit
before he nudged the horn, and after too—
where be your gibes now, your gambols, young buck?

That was when he caught my scent and snorted,
and blew the way that means stand back in moose.
I'm Polonius, hidden by a tree,
I feared, as Hamlet strode my way, head down.
But no. Such madness comes mostly in the fall.

This was spring. The clownish buck, winter-killed,
was nothing. So the bull, un-Hamlet-like,
just stopped, and the audience, which was trees
and grasses and flowers, began to breathe
again, and the stage, littered with corpses

historical, became in fact the world,
or the earth, at least, where I was a man
who waited, then left, the buck's skull in hand.
On the back wall of the shed, quite a few hang,
allusive, each one mocking its own grin.

# Moose Poem

*"Finally I question the fairness—a fucking moose poem by
Robert Wrigley? Jeezus."*

—Found on a blog at
http://mistressofmyfate.blogspot.com, now vanished

Having written, I confess, more than one in which a moose is
but none in which a moose is fucking, I must come
to the conclusion that the use of such a fine, time-honored, and tabooed
locution is nothing more than a lazy adjective. How sad.

Not for me, but for the moose, whom I have
simply scratching his snout on a deer skull's skeletal antler
and contemplating the Shakespearean fates of us all,
or, though obsessed with procreating, not at the moment doing so.

The word's just a synonym for *damned* (or, given the spelling
of Jesus, perhaps *danged*), therefore I question the fairness too, directly.
What did our noble ungulate to you, mistress? This is no doofussy
Bullwinkle, but a thousand-pound "American Archangel,"

in Anne Sexton's description. His mate's a cow seven feet tall
at the brow. Imagine that, *and* what prodigious mating they might make.
Or else don't, which I suspect you would not care to do anyway.
It's the moose, after all, a critter. One might as well speak of a flea.

How could such a poem as *that* be done? A mouse? A louse?
Or more: a frigate pelican? a frigging snake in a trough at Taormina?
a grazer big as a house? Each one an albatross, not at all like ourselves.
Fate, Jesus, fate. Mistress, this snit of ours may well *be* about what's fair.

Just the two of us: I who admit writing more than one poem in which
there's a moose, and you, how little your denial of him is.

## Sombrero Cowboy

Little dumpling, art thou tender?
Notice how the moose's dewlap's asway
and casts a pendular shadow.
Daylight is a clock this way.

Honestly, I think if I could ride a moose
I'd be a happier man, I do.
Just sidle up, saddle up, a rodeo sideshow:
I'd canter proud while the cows go moo.

As for you, hunk of dough in a broth
of skin and salt, tell me, where O
where would you find such a cowboy
as I am, with my moose, and my sombrero?

## Against Nostalgia

It's not the rich man, all business and BMW,
no, no, not him, but me, said he, though he was me
in the time of which we speak, we do.

Ooo, he was galled in the flesh, played plum out, depleted
so happily he could not believe he was the me
he'd dreamed of being. He watched the sweets he'd sweeted

as she gardened the garden spot he'd turned in the nude—
she, that is, not he, or the him that was me;
no, no, it was she—seeding and seeded nude and so unlewd

he sat and stroked his belly and murmured most fecundly
the pure satisfaction of all. To him as well as to me,
though more me, let's admit, and him secondly.

Though he wondered at the wonder of it, as I do too—me,
I mean, wondering who she loved or loves more, that we
we were, that he who was him, and now is me.

# Nessun Compresso in Difesa della Terra

*Florence, October 2007*

Sacred music wafts a cappella from second-story windows,
open late this balmy autumn night: a choir of young women,
one of whom probably did not wield the can of spray paint
that emblazoned this graffito across a wall along the Borgo Pinti.
My wife has bought a bottle of wine with two paper cups
from a trattoria nearby. In the lee of the curb
we sit, elbow to elbow in the one empty space among dozens
of Vespas. God, of course, is great. Dinner was too.
Insalata di trippa, coniglio farcito, et passata di peperoni gialli.
Never having spoken to the butcher next door, I feel
I've come to know him nevertheless, his once-a-day nod to me
before he leers at my wife's backside. Such work as his,
I trust, will never be done. As for the planet here,
though it is mostly stone and old, still from its softer places
come yellow peppers Platonically perfect,
the vast rubbery and complicated digestive tracts
of cows, and the tender hindquarters of rabbits.
Tomorrow, a short flight to Amsterdam, long to Seattle,
short again to Idaho, over Greenland, subarctic Canada,
the Rockies, and the Cascades twice. Only now,
music stopped, the young women come in twos
and threes out the door, laughing and talking,
each sound another kind of song. Some notice us
and smile (*buona notte, buona notte*),
though none of them acknowledges the manifesto on the wall,
nor the anarchist symbol—a bloody *A* within a circle—
but light their cigarettes, walk or buzz away on wheels,
and disappear over the face, which is also beautiful, of the earth.

# ACKNOWLEDGMENTS

*The Atlantic Monthly*: Cemetery Moles
BigCityLit.com: After a Rainstorm; Progress
*Café Solo*: Misunderstanding
*Ecotone*: A Rumor of Bears; Hailstorm in the Mountains
*Five Points*: Ashtray in the Snow
*Fugue*: Fraternity
*Georgia Review*: Hourglass
*Gulf Stream*: But He Did
*Hampden-Sydney Poetry Review*: Letting Go
*High Desert Journal*: Old Bucket
*Hudson Review*: Finding a Bible in an Abandoned Cabin
*Kenyon Review*: Yorick
*Knockout*: Cream
*Little Star*: Campfire; Every Night the Long Swim
*Margie*: Beautiful Country; What the Night Horse Runs From
*Meridian*: Lichen
*New Ohio Review*: Anthropomorphic Duck
*New South*: Hay Day
*The New Yorker*: Exxon; I Like the Wind
*Northwest Review*: County; Poor Priscilla
*Orion*: Duff
*Ploughshares*: Night Walk
*Poetry*: A Lock of Her Hair; Do Not Go; "Little Prick"; Moose Poem
*Poetry International*: Night Music
*Shenandoah*: Full Moon and Horse; Miss June, 1971
Slate.com: Wait
*Smartish Pace*: At a Cabin in the Woods
*Southern Poetry Review*: Soap
*Virginia Quarterly Review*: None Shall Sleep; Responsibility
*Willow Springs*: Memoir; They Are Bidden
*The Yale Review*: Sisyphus Bee; What Is Yellow About the Yellow Pine?

"Lichen" appeared in *Pushcart Prize XXXIII: Best of the Small Presses*, 2009.
"Beautiful Country" appeared in *Pushcart Prize XXXIV: Best of the Small Presses*, 2010.
"What Is Yellow About the Yellow Pine?" was printed as an Armfield Broadside, at the University of North Carolina–Chapel Hill.

Matt Valentine

Robert Wrigley's previous books include *Lives of the Animals*, winner of the Poets' Prize; *Reign of Snakes*, which won the Kingsley Tufts Award; and *In the Bank of Beautiful Sins*, which was awarded the San Francisco Poetry Center Book Award. He lives with his wife, the writer Kim Barnes, in the woods near Moscow, Idaho.

# PENGUIN POETS